IDYLLS OF BEING

Poems by Melvin Litton

Stubborn Mule Press
Devil's Elbow, MO
stubbornmulepress.com

Copyright (c) Melvin Litton, 2018
First Edition 1 3 5 7 9 10 8 6 4 2
ISBN: 978-1-946642-73-8
LCCN: 2018911220

Design, edits and layout: Jeanette Powers
Cover image: Melvin Litton
Interior images: Karl Ramberg
Author photo: Debra Litton
All rights reserved. No part of this publication may be reproduced or transmitted in any form or by any means, electronic or mechanical, including photocopying, recording or by info retrieval system, without prior written permission from the author.

Special thanks to Stubborn Mule Press and particularly poet / editors Jeanette Powers and Jason Ryberg for putting this all together and making it happen.

And ever grateful to my old friend, artist / sculptor Karl Ramberg, for contributing the prints for the poems herein.

The cover image is the author's sketch of Kansas sculptor Pete Felten, Hays, KS (c. Autumn 1973).

IDYLLS OF BEING

While idylls typically evoke airy pastoral themes, these root to an older, tragic tradition. Threads of man, elements, and seasons play in and out, weaving quest, mortality, landscape, and dream in four poems penned over forty years ago then boxed away, now unearthed, dusted off, and let to breathe…

Old Lives / 1

The Woodsman's Tale / 15

Wind Cry / 45

Death Psalm / 71

IDYLLS OF BEING

For my beloved sisters, Barbara and Nancy, women of spirit, grace, and beauty. Gone too soon, forever dear to my heart...

Druid by Karl Ramberg

OLD LIVES

I.

A subtle existence upon the wold,
the wolf knows loneliness the same as
an old woman. My orchard bears fruit,
but with an agony of thorns on the cross,
a painful birth and is always so…

A savage of middle night and morning
cloaked in flannel instead of mammal skins,
I count no coups, merely thoughts.
A serpent possessed of fine poison,
yet no fangs for delivery. My life tragically
moored with the worms beneath the sun.
No fields, nor beasts, only my labor to sow,
I harvest forms spiced with color
and variance of emotions, like storms,
and lastly, death. I await spring and new
blood, and a sword to battle the adversity
which shadows like a brother…

And in the East, to the valley of all origin,
where night and morning wed beneath the
physics of evolution, the day unfolds. But with
insufficient heat to move this flesh whose passions
wane and still. Empty, I flee the feist of present-time
to confront the terrible specters caterwauling from
the past, where each word is voiced in the rapt,
vertiginous speech of those whose light
has long faded beyond the curtain…

II.

The wind seeks new borders,
flees the steppe warriors of the North
to settle its wings upon the lees
and timber of my valley...

It rains unseen...
Diaphanous mists drift over fields where
angry ghost fog hangs haunting the gullies
like white death of cannons fired in silence,
while beyond, through the bottoms, hay bales
lay ungathered like soldier lads at Antietam...

It rains unseen...
A moist, vaporous breath enfolds, clogging the
distance, the scene contained, entranced, mystic.
Here a Red-tail Hawk rolls and searches,
mesmerizing through the liquid sky.
Colors deep like water, of dimension,
geometry, and hue, their essence ensconced
in finite grays, browns, yellows, russets, and
greens, like leaves in Appalachian coal towns.

Umber silhouettes soften the angles while
burnt grass and rotted wood incense the hollows.
The entire scene painted in muted oils and lacquered
mists as if imported like the pheasant from Asia to
bestow ancient riches and metaphor...

It rains unseen…
In the rude evening hogs rut and feed,
stirring mud and feces like in a Spanish still-life
where peasants stomp their feet in vatted grapes…

Dusk deepens like lines of ink
writhing across the page as the night fox
emerges from crevices of the dark, sculpted land.
Now the moon serves witness to the lowly shadow
of the sun and through the window I perceive
the ghost image of a candle and rush
to my old friend, the fire, who comforts me
with stories of Old Lives on the long savannahs
and cold tundras of lost history…

III.

With thoughts of winter I climb the stairs
to search quilted warmth instead
of cool sheets and sex…

Yet tonight my mistress sleep yields no pleasure,
leaves me longing for her semblance at the window.
I turn from her cold eyes and walk the darkness
as the wick flame illumines my passage
and sets the furtive shadows dancing.
Outside, the moon whispers veiled light,
the hand that holds it forth forever hidden
like the distance through the rain…

Why to the heavens plead?
Why should infinity beckon one
Whose utter origins stalk each breath?
The mystery that buoys the moon and suspends my life,
to what end? That I should lie alone and supine,
a corpse, a cool light, my flesh eclipsed with the owl and
serpent, death rendering all forms into the same pale
sculpture?

Time-scorned, mocked, so that my progeny should one
day visit my bones and call to me:

> *Old Skullman! Still and silent warrior!*
> *You suffer the delirium of too much sleep...*

And further presume of me with callow intellect:

> *What colored visions danced within?*
> *Were you medieval or Neolithic man?*
> *Were you soldier or scholar?*
> *Did knowledge abound in that cavity?*
> *Were you a brooding man, insular and heroic,*
> *scarred by wounds of inner battle, leaving long*
> *gashes furrowed upon your brow and bloodstains*
> *beneath your eyes? Did you stare in common with*
> *the idiot and drunkard, the crippled and feeble,*
> *share their admonition and rejection,*
> *their shame and tragedy? Did you cry and curse*
> *at the mass adulation of fools? Were you poet,*
> *prophet, or beggar...or a prince of fools?*

*Did that two-faced goddess, Reason, the one of
golden hair, take your youth and teach you the
laws of pleasure, of arrogant gain, bravado, and
senseless quests? Did she have you lusting for the
knowledge of her flesh then abandon you for one
younger and of fatter purse?
Tempting, jealous, frivolous, and haughty, did
she redden your eyes and leave you stumbling
blind, begging redemption?
Skullman! Old mystery!
If you could speak, what words would echo
from the ether's lexicon?*

You child, talk to me of madness and existence?
You wade shallow waters and I have swum with
leviathan. Spirits are not new to me…

IV.

To the Northwest, perilous drums of violent
summer rains rumbled as lowering disquietudes
which augured tornadoes echoed from the South.
The sun stroked the panorama, knelling
beneath Red Cloud's mighty arm while
Mankato's thunderous spirit stormed in nemesis
over the land.
Mankato! Red Cloud! Near and mythic, I was born
amid reverberations of their ghostly warring…

In winter, stalked cane leaned tee-peed
in the fields, snow-skins of white buffalo
covering the sheaves to shed the cold
from my inner warmth where
I squatted in savage peace…

And nights beneath the summer's purple
sky, vertigo induced by the fathomless depths,
dizzied by the avid pull of oceanic beauty and death,
my heart unbidden by sorrow grasped the infinite, my
spirit certain. I harvested fireflies in the evenings,
their illuminations another cosmos.
The gods reigned the heavens, and I the earth…

But it happened, as happens with all.
Suddenly the door to the wind sprung open
and my questions could no longer be answered…

I lay in a glen of young elms, their swaying
shoots anchored in the moist May soil, and
watched feathery clouds whiff overhead, traced
by sun-tinted swallow wings. I teased yet feared
the shadow man who stood beyond the barn,
appearing midway after lunch and before the call
to dinner, then grew the full span towards the creek
and became the night. I climbed the sapling elms
and sailed against zealous winds, an unwary child
about to fall and receive broken dreams…

Since that day I have chased shades of beauty,
flesh, and poetry, luckless as a fiddle without a bow…

No longer have I the gaiety of a lark,
though I wish, nor the certitude of a young
and fallow mind. The philosopher's mastery
of situations, his acrobatics with past, future,
and distance, no – nor a mathematician's grasp
of vague, ineffable calculus. Madness eludes me,
intuition I distrust, leading more often to chaos.
The elliptical yo-yoing of conversation bores me.
And religion would damn me to fits of sanctity
and shame. I haven't the courage to say
"I do," nor sufficient guilt to confess "I did."
So what is there to hold me but the will
of music, magic, and woman?

V.

As the moon and her influence visit the dun
wood an incessant pulse gnaws at my fingertips
to caress my guitar and hatch the yolk of melody.
Upon the dappled wall my vision defines an apparition
that claws and chants of abeyant forms.
My calloused fingers hunger for their prey
like a wolf pack searching through the far night,
wanting the other, the nameless, to receive its
pitch and grace…

A stallion softly neighs across the pasture.
My flesh is warmed. Four and twenty years I
have walked the earth, yet part of me has slept,
that which is born bereft, the orphaned soul
of each generation...

I have slashed through jungles and clove waters
of the Aegean, marched with Roman legions,
and fallen in the desert. I've bled my life into the
Tigris and the Mississippi, roamed the valleys of Crete
and Kansas, and fled the night of a hundred separate
centuries...

Always in moments of love I have such visions...

And who is not my father?
Is not all substance an experience of itself?
Honey its sweetness; the mind its thought,
and all thoughts mere ideas of sweetness, cold, sorrow,
delight, the whole gathered like driftwood on a beach
for the flaming pyre to disseminate through measure of
ocean, continents, and space?
We bear the time-print of all origin, genetics of
fantastic depth, nebular birth and galactic wounds, the
mineral asters of Precambrian seas, exuberant fruit of
the Pleistocene, of reptilian obsessions, devils, gods,
creatures of Dostoyevsky, warriors of Stonehenge and
the Crusades. Beneath the sanguine sky and fathoms of
death surfaces again and again,
no matter how faint the last attenuated cry,

"Must live, must live, must live..."

Who is not my father?

I reach into my gut to seek the future, gripping each
moment as it occurs, that the potentialities of moon
and demon, this pitiable flesh and nothingness be
experienced and metaphysically endured, that the lost
wax of visual divinities be granted the finality
of bronze. I stand within this ghost land of fleeting
atmospheres inhabited solely by native cedar masking
the stone and iron-fenced plots of our fathers' graves,
that this twilight be made known and charted,
for it is in the gut that vignettes of mind and heart merge
and are threshed beneath the milestone of sleepless
nights and labored days, producing the narrative of
hidden forces, dark mysteries of the moon's lost surface,
and the shared veins of blood, sperm, spleen, and soil
marking the inheritance of the human soul...

VI.

A lone figure within the diorama of night,
Saturnine with pains of mortality, life's nexus,
and this frigid flesh, this impotence that binds
the dust of our unborn, calling wild yet mute,
drawn to the cool light, the shadow of our earth,
drawn into a sea of storms, this cavity that bears
no child save silence...

A single breaker moistens Africa's bony shore.
The wind rustles then rests, breathless, captive
in lapsed ballon. Autumn returns the self to my
flesh as dawn transcends opacity with a gray,
monochrome translucence that advances
briefly then awaits...

The night's contagious richness stills the sun's
ingress as the heart ingests motes of song
refracted through all memory. Focused on this
temporal plane, a spirit seemingly risen from
an old borrow, a ruin of stone, its brumal breath
formed in echo of my father's birth, an animism
chorused in rivers, clouds, and fiery coals...

As scents of old tributaries become
known again at flood stage, fruits from
thickets and arbors caught in its savage grip,
so the quintessence of unrecalled ancestry
answers the saturation of our mortal currents

and a man becomes the cynosure as his soul rages above
blood tide, more sentient than perfervid flesh, battling a
maelstrom of unveiled reflections...

A cognitive presence imbues my shadow's form,
a tangential vernacular evolving at the periphery of
consciousness, an avatar which is and is not the self...

>*From the East I journeyed, frail*
>*substance upon a long, shadowed*

*path glazed by sun and dew, seeking
my shadow as a virgin seeks promise.
For a moment I stood achieved, the
polestar of creation, a triumph brief
and deceiving, for my substance and
energies soon waned. I journeyed West,
again seeking my shadow cast behind,
growing long and mysterious within
the vesperal cloak until that greater
shadow consumed my substance...*

Vain embers of anxiety flare in my heart,
this message a vile anchor to the vessel of
my thoughts: Am I not the pilgrim returned
from Mecca via the river Acheron, transfixed
by dire knowledge of our shared demise?
Of fate I expect nothing but the life of a
flameless dragon, hunted and haunted.
The weeds will grow tall upon my grave...

*You are Narcissus crying wolf,
frightened of burning life and age,
a fool to long for immortality of form
over substance, ignorant of deities
within your reach. Gods subject to
age and death, yet gods no less.
And of your father's memory
you are ignorant as well.
Look! The sun is risen!
Its hand brings forth the seed of life,
awakens moist, wanton procreation,*

*and forms the trees, great bones of
fibrous statuary, to commemorate the
ancient coupling of flesh and spirit.
The pollen of your life falls unwedded
beyond the flower and fails to fructify
like an incubus cast out of dreams.
Wonder that Dionysian blood should anger
and boil within lax Lutheran flesh?
This quandary of submissiveness, leave it!
The only certain death is life suborned,
   shamed, and subdued...*

The damp, lethargic night cowers aside
the stallion's celerity as the aura of ancient
amplitudes forms the morning's first light.
I cast my last draught of energy into its
opulent wave like a harpoon into Leviathan,
seeking to rein in my mad inertia and doubt,
forsaking the night, cruel mistress, my sleepless
soliloquy, for the day, to explore a further river
and vision and there discern a path...
The wind cries through the crannies,
depositing tremolos of old madrigals,
probing the senses with intoxicants
and reckless wonder...
I surrender like a savage entering
the Sun Dance, receiving in its entirety
the half-vision that has haunted me since
I was a child...

His face glows with lines of vibrant
poetics haloed by the pale ochre of
memory, his brow etched by tragedy
and long experience of a visceral heart,
his undulant voice expressing now the
thunder, now the gentle patter of the rain.
Old as a Druid and mutable as a flood,
his lineage as much of the sea as the prairie,
his hands in the mold of a dayworker or peasant,
the Irish, German, night and wolf, warm his blood.

He is a Nordic ghost, a Cheyenne son,
the timeless beast whose source and border
lies beyond and within that part of each
which falls to the soil and rises in the seed,
which survives self-murder to enter the life of a son,
which haunts the gibbet and crossroad,
paring agony from one flesh to another
as the wind carries eluvium and desecration
to regions of innocence…

Call him Old Lives, the culminated longings
And passions of a species, our fervent memory
scintillating off snow mountains and far deserts,
man returned to self and soul,
progenitor of unresolved poetry…

Wolf Cairn by Karl Ramberg

THE WOODMAN'S TALE

"A voice between silence and a shadow's sigh,
  neither here nor there, above nor below,
  I am Mary's spirit humming, her unfettered soul.
Between the grass and beneath the starry sky,
  in the fruit of the tree that bears the seed
    and still my Daniel's love,
      and am the tree and too the seed,
    and too the breeze which breeds the seed...
I was Mary's body once, but died and swept away,
    and it was night and now is day,
      morning for Daniel who still lives lonely...
Gone so soon our together hours within the world,
  and I am mourning, without a whimper or a tear...
    Can life be less and mere for memory?
    Though my heart died, my love has pulse,
      and I am mind-soul memory...
Quiet then my love moves without, no part of gone
  or dead, but waiting yet, as Daniel's time is yet,
    and I am watching for his time to end,
    near in wait, wanting when our souls will blend.
  As our love is yet, I am yet, both distant and near,
    somewhere between longing and waiting,
      between night and day, dusk and dawn..."

Frolic of Spring…

A robin chirrups, singing far and nigh, calling
wrens, larks, swallows, redwings, driven in
droves, echoing through the mist where the
distance yields to rushing throngs of winged
spirits, hovering by, fluttering to nest in
their old north homes atop the trees…

The Robin's song answers to the blissful awakening
of a silver dawn pouring in through the window
bright on the woodsman's eyes.
He breathes good air, breaking his mouth to yawn,
*"Ah, the sun, the sun…still summons my flesh
and bone, I'll not deny…"* his thoughts as he
moves to meet the morning fully…

Coffee brewed thick and black, he clasps
his hands prayerful about the cup and sips,
sniffing the rich steam odor, letting
the warmth seep to his far bones…
Soothed, he strikes a flame to light his pipe…

Outside…following the morning glaze,
the woodsman licks the melting sap of a budding
maple, looks to his boots mud-caked by the morning
wet rooting to the good earth…flexes his gnarly
limbs, now drawing straight, stands like the
maple, leans to the wind and goes to chore…

But beyond…to the bluing sky, woods, grass, and
creek, life is astir even before the woodsman.
The Old Mother spins and weaves new garments,
sprouting buds on trees, bushes, flowers…
kindling, lusting, bearing, nourishing life,
thaws the dormant turf to a greening pasture
where a young bull-calf snorts, frisking to a notion.
Swiftly but gently her fingers tickle stillness
to motion, set little ones to play, to grow and
listen and to watch as their elders display
the enduring patterns of their first
mornings, their days and lives…

Pacing the path winding low through
the mottled green near the creek,
a wolf leaps in lambent flow, silent
as the waters, then darts handsomely
out of a thicket, hunting a fresh kill…
Behind him, no more than shooting distance,
his mate and cubs, caved innocents lately
born to a lean custom, not yet knowing,
seeking or wanting the wind…not yet,
only warmth, like suckling lambs
till age concedes their feral form…

The wolf, poised in delicate balance, blends
with shape and shadow, tasting his senses,
listening to the grass, nips the air, asking,
then slows, utterly still, aslant the pawned rabbit.

He crouches, bristling low, muzzles his thirst and
eases forth like a mountaineer nearing a slick
summit, placing each paw with deft care,
lowering further like a snake, slithering…then
like an arrow he strikes the rabbit with knifed teeth,
quickly muffling its torrid, shrill scream…then
trances on, head up, keen-eyed, running in
quiet lope, the limp prey dangling from his jaws,
blood dripping to blue violets underneath.
Into the narrow den, darkly hidden, the wolf
slouches, granting its eager members
their first eating of flesh amid
their last whimper for milk…

Theirs, an unlikely Easter…

Tolling…distant bells of the village church sound
through the morning as the spinster faithfully
saunters to prayer, a scowling devout goaded
on by others funneling piously to hear a stately
posture brim the word, "On the third day He arose
and walked again among his flock," with rising fervor,
"Christ our Savior who promised life eternal!
All lambs in a thick of wolves…and He our
Shepherd…" at last calmly folding his hands,
"Dear Lord, let us pray…"

The woodsman digs the old earth, hoeing
and working the soil to plant his garden.

He too hears the tolling, thinking,
"No Easter this year...Mary gone..."
No Easter, no resurrection, the woodsman
works his garden, the soil black-rick, smelling
of molding straw and old fruits...
He leans and grips the handle in thought,
remembers the *"wolves...lambs...the savoir..."*
looks to the morning, believes only in the morning,
and speaks, *"The wolf preys on the lamb and
God is slayer of man...He took Mary..."*
Again to the soil, mixing memories with the
fond black dirt where grub-worms gnaw
and earthworms furrow, returning
flesh and thought to the soil...

The youth's boot...blurs...kicks the dust,
he crosses the dew grass and stamps
to her door...he knocks, calling,
"Maireee...!" wondering how his voice sounds.
"Coming, Daniel..." appearing sweetly in
curtsy and smile, cradling a basket.
"Is that my Easter basket?"
"Uhmmm, sort of...it's our lunch," adding
brightly, "They'll be gone all day..."
"Did you tell them?"
"I told them I was sick..." betraying an
impish grin.
"Now Mary, the truth...always tell the truth."
"But," she mocks, "they think I'm too young."

"No, none too young, but all too soon…too old."
"Oh Daniel…you…" …a kiss…and both
off running, laughing to the morning…

Thunder and their quick leaping echo the
notion of clouds lowering, shading the sky,
soon forming a storm, a cloudburst…
The morning shower falls abrupt and the Old
Mother answers to the valley's thirst as flowering
petals open, cupped to capture the beaded rain
flowing to each tender root and spear…

Nearby…in innocent frolic on damp grass,
the lovers suddenly cast their eyes,
"It's raining, Daniel…"
"That it is, Mary. Here, up now, best into
the orchard before we catch our death…"
Knowing of a better place to lie, he leads
her running under hanging branches
to dry warm blossoms in first bloom.
"Oh Daniel, we're soaked through!"
"All the better to cover passion's sweat."
"Daniel, you…you're a rogue…"
"Ay, you the rose…I the rogue, and more,
I'm the thorn to your fragrant petal…
soon to prick its velvet softness…"
"Daniel, no…" she pleads, "not now…"
"I'm sorry, Mary…here, stay close…"
embracing gently to calm their want,
certain their love is growing…

But beneath the branches no passion sweat,
  Mary weeps while Daniel strokes her hair,
    speaking softly, yet restless, urgent…
"Mary, I need more than Sunday mornings and
    chance nights…I need you with me always…"
He rolls to his back to still his desperate longing,
  to grip, take, merge…but no, dries his emotion
  and need, his lips breaking in bitter sigh,
"Life…a brier wreath of man and woman
    twined in grief…"
  "Oh Daniel, your head is cloudy."
  "No, Mary…my heart…"

The same, the woodsman's heart beats low
  looking to his garden quickly sown, thinking,
    "Half again as much as last year…"

Mary points to the sky, "Look, Daniel, it's clearing!"
  The heavens open and shoo the clouds…plants
    green to the sunlight beaming down as sheer
      as through a prism, shedding a high rainbow
      of iridescence like an artist's hand across a
    canvas, granting color and beauty, arched high
    above fields of corn, wheat, and barley…
      the blessed sun, altar to the farms
    and pastures gracing the valley…

The lovers gone…others, young rascals, run
  ranting through the orchard, anxious for the

coming harvest, shouting out color and kind,
"*White! Pink! Red…! Peach! Apple! Cherry…!*"
claiming each budded fruit by name…

The woodsman searches his cabin,
    the wolves listen, waiting…
The youngsters dream of fruit, also waiting…
      the woodsman searches…the lovers dance…
The woodsman finds her locket and weeps…

Daniel picks a buttercup for Mary,
    yellow petals reflecting her fair glow…

Summer Longing…

The day hollers, "Hey'ya, Butchie!"
    "Call me 'Butchie' once't more, Clem –"
      "Whatcha got for bait?"
    "Earthworms…"
      "Grasshoppers 'er better."
    "Not so, earthworms is."
      "Aw Butchie…*Ouch!*" Clem hops
    holding his shin while Butch runs
      laughing to the catfish hole…
    "I git you, Butch Harold…dang I will…!"

Beyond range of fist or foot Butch slides
down the muddy bank, hooks his worm and
tosses the line in wait for Clem, smiling,
    watching the bobber lap the current…

"Better you hurry, Clem, else I'll catch
all the fish…'n eat 'em too!"

The woodsman bends, weeding his garden,
the day lays heavy on his shoulders,
tired muscles strain, tighten, and flex
beneath the woolen flannel, red threads
frayed white at cuff and collar to fit his work.
Standing, he gasps for breath, eyes stinging from
sweat, lips parched, grabs his handkerchief
and wipes his brow wrinkled not from
frowning but by thought and sun.
He spreads a broad hand through matted hair,
mostly gray, black at the temples, curling to
his neck ridged by bitter winds and the
blistering sun…so too his ruddy face,
years etched in runic lines on
chiseled cheeks, eyes, and brow…

The woodsman stares evenly at the day, wishing,
"I could taste a cool breeze or hook a squirmin'
worm, maybe point the sun the other way…"
The woodsman stares, his aquiline nose sniffing
hoed earth and ripe fruit into his thoughts,
"Long ago I wrung pleasure from such a day…"
He stares off and away, eyes fixed on heat
waves rippling through the distant green,
undulating beneath blue-gray sky, old dust
blowing, settling in muddy reams on his arms.
He kneels to fondle a blighted tomato, cursing,

"Damned worms…" rests his large hands,
sinewed to grip the land, scarred by
scythe and ax, broken and calloused
from picking the fruit and taking the toil.
Rests his hands in stare at the hard old land,
then shoulders his rifle and walks
to the woods, hunting wolf…

The wolves loll in the shade, panting cool,
an old male and mate, knowing, listening,
instincts calm, pacing the silent creek…

Butch falls to the water, thinking…*Clem pushed me!*
water warm and mossy, but cool where catfish go,
Butch thinking…*Cold!* Clem falling too, knees to
the grass, laughing as Butch surfaces, spits and
yells, "Clem, ya rat! Jus' wait ta I catch
you, Clem! Ya smit-shit! Clem…!"

The woodsman steps over a fallen limb and
stands searching, eyes intent, staring evenly…

Suddenly alert to those keen eyes the boys
scramble forth like young hounds to their
master's feet, licking the very air…
"Yessir!" "Yessur!" "We's fishin'"
"Yep, catfish" – they both affirm,
and yet again, "Fishin'…yessur…"

The woodsman stands towering above the pair
   piping away like squirrels before a wolf in
     hope their chatter saves them from his fangs.
He stares down, shadow covering both, thinking,
*Yeah…uh huh…*and answers in knowing drawl,
   "You boys gonna catch more ticks than fish
     wrestlin' in the grass there…"
        Demanding, "You know that?"
They nod in earnest, "Yessir!" then
   quietly, now chastened, "Yessur…"
"Fishin'…yeah, well…" the woodsman casts
   his steel-gray eyes, mulling the moment,
     "If I's fishin' catfish…I'd try down
        yonder there where that old dead oak
           sprawls out over the water…"
"Oh-h-h…thanks, Mister Daniel!"
   "Yessir , we'll catch 'em! Yessur, thanks…"
Backing away, glad to escape a tanning,
   they turn in rush for their poles, whispering,
   "That's ol' Mister Daniel…"
     "I know, Clem…fished with him once…"
His eyes widening, he thrusts a finger in
   Clem's face and shouts, "An' he tol'
     me earthworms is better'n grasshoppers!"
"Aw Butchie…*uh-oh*…" hushing his friend,
   "…he's still eyin' us…"

The woodsman regards the boys' antics and smiles,
   recalling his and Mary's two sons…then sobers,

both lost to the war, further he dare not look...
Gone...just gone... he shifts his gaze to the creek,
noting niche and fork, treads on, hunting wolf...

They rest in the shade, the old male and mate,
panting cool, lapping water cool, laying low,
instincts calm, listening in the silent creek...

The woodsman wonders... *Where?*
Stares to the north grove where the trees thin,
less cover, but better breeze and cool shade.
Senses the day loom lower and breathes...
Yeah...to the north grove...

The woodsman knows the day, believes in
the day, but doubts each night in witness
of familiar shades lengthening to the grave...
He steps quiet, patient...for now is day and summer,
dust rises in swirling gusts borne on hot winds
forcing back his breath, lips dry-parched from
whetted thirst like raw passion unappeased
till all sleep sated in their black earth home.
Night waits as day blazes, waits in still calm for
the coming storm, muffled in the distance,
rumbling as it rolls up in thunderous blast,
crushing over and streaking down, framing
earth-flesh-sky...frightening mare and colt,
flooding draws, creeks, and wells with muddy
waters gushing from unstaunched wounds...

As the violence of summer and too a maiden's
    passion must go beyond pleasure to pain,
        so the earth seeks fire thrusting to her soil,
    heart trembling as she quakes beneath rife
winds wrenching the prized loam through spiraling
clouds of dark thunder powered by her gift-giving,
    taken to give back, swollen deep in her warmth
        and bowels till the searing pain bursts to
    pleasure overflowing, she screams, *"I love!"*
        She knows his heat, she gave it flame,
            clutching, rapt in damp smolder…

    They part, face the face, passion subsiding,
        she whispers, "I love you, Daniel…"
            "And I you, Mary…"

The woodsman knows that night is for loving,
    and dying, and day in summer is for harvest,
*even to kill…*thinking this, he leans to a tree,
    gaining breath, temples throbbing, eyes
        squinting to the shade, asking, *Where…?*

    There, in the brush, panting calm, moving slow…
The woodsman straightens, searching, eyes intent,
    stares evenly and aims, squeezing the trigger…

    The death-shot echoes, exploding the day
        as the wolf spins, hitting the ground, biting
            at the wound, the burning flesh, tasting blood,

his own…wanting cool from the fiery pain…
now cold up his spine to dimming eyes…
drops his head, stiffens and dies…

A crow cries…the she-wolf runs crazed,
a wild thing, widowed and fanged with terror,
snapping at the trees and air, snarling her
sorrow to the heat that hid the man scent
too heavy to carry without a breeze,
so her mate, lax, unwary, is killed…

The woodsman squats by the wolf, draws
his knife to claim the ears and speaks,
"It's been awhile…eh, ol' wolf…?
You trackin' my traps, me trackin' you…
S'pose you had a right, more your woods 'n mine.
Yeah, you had right, but I got you all the same.
Though always thought you'd outlast me…"
He grips the ears and stands, notes the worn teeth
and the gray muzzle, "Ol' wolf, didn't know
you's so old…" thinking…*Doubt you
were ready…but bet you believed.
Yeah, you knew I's comin'…*

The woodsman raises his gaze to the sky,
asking…sees in the revolving clouds his
own features vaguely form then gradually
evolve into a great wolf head staring down…
His thoughts return to his youth…once a

student of books, an actor in love, a wry poet,
then shed it all to come to the woods and
love a woman truly…and had till lately,
now having only the woods to love….
And the woodsman knows, for his tears tell
him well, that part of what sustained him
was the wolf killed by his hand this day…

Longing streams from his weary eyes
as blood drips from the bounty ears…
The woodsman looks to the gift of the wolf,
the life he has taken, to the day, its gift of warmth
and light, to the green trees and cool water,
with thoughts of all life has given…
Given him strong arms which long ago
this day held her trembling young flesh,
touching, taking her innocence shaken…
Of all gifts life had given he had never taken
more than from her, and the woodsman
asks between quickened breaths,
"Did I give to you..? Mary…?
Did I love thee well…?"

Knowing that day, this hard day,
was for killing…but also for longing,
for day is long and the tale day speaks is
measured only by the length of longing,
and the length of longing is the length
of life…this he knows and believes…

The woodsman harnesses Jed and
Jude and hitches the wagon, yelling,
"Whoa! Ya cursed fools...ya gul-dern
mules...Whoa!" then knees Jude to
tighten the girth...all secure, mounts
the buckboard and snaps the reins,
"Hae-ya!" and heads for the village...

He knows of his longing...longing to give,
but knows there is no one...*all gone, just gone...*
The woodsman turns his thoughts to the wheels
turning over the dust while his mind turns
tumbling through measure of time and distance,
to whistled melodies and fiddle tunes from
dances and picnics...all the bitter-sweet
memories of long-gone days...

The wagon rolls a tumble-weed aside, wheels
turning, churning the dust settling to the
edge where grass awaits a breeze to take
his mind-dust rushing to the meadow of
everlasting dream, to youth and love,
where Daniel cradles Mary's head,
ever tender and dear, sharing his urgent
desire as she aches, arching to the same,
as a rainbow to the sky, to him, as a mother
gives milk, to him...her breasts, her warmth,
her all she trusts to him...woman arching,
receiving...man taking, entering, whispering,

"I love...love ..." their rhythms flowing,
    parting in sigh to lily blossoms next to
    them, their love apt and pure as the same...

The woodsman haws his mules toward the village
    past fields of grain and golden harvest where
    rustling reeds fall before scythe and sickle,
    the steady tug of horse and man, admiring
    all the ripe growth nourished of the soil,
    black-rich, of old fruits and rotting straw,
    grain thrashed from sheaths bound in twine...

Eying the harvest, he dreams of hot-buttered
    bread, of sweet corn dripping the same,
    of sucking juices from a tomato's lush fruit,
    and meat roasted brown set savorily on a table...
He dreams of the first frost when he can taste again
    the soothing air, turn from the furnacing heat
    and face the chill, crystalline beauty that
    breathes though an autumn evening...

The woodsman grips the reins, pulling long,
    "Who-o-a...there!" eases back, "Whoa boys..."
    halts his team before *Tamm's General Store,*
    lashes reins to post, tightens the knot,
    then steps up, greeted as he enters...
    "Good day, Daniel!"
        "Howdy, Ira..."
    "She's hellish hot, ain't she?"

"Sure is…hotter'n a potbelly in winter."
"Yep…uh-huh-he-he…" chuckling, "Yep,
not far off, no, not a'tall. Say now,
you be wantin' a soda, Daniel?"
"No, Ira…not today …don't truly feel
right from the heat. Just some bacon
'n flour…doubt a soda would agree…"
"That's quite alright. Why here…" leans to the
counter, "What you got there?"
"Oh, finally bagged that ol' wolf…" tosses
down the ears, "though I don't know,
may have been the heat got 'im first."
"Well, looks like you finished 'im, Daniel. Yep,
you surely did…"
"Yeah…" the woodsman bites his lip,
wondering *who got who…*

The boys, Clem and Butch, skip down the road,
mindless of the heat, kicking at their
shadows dangling from the sun.
Butch teases, "Clem loves Janey Haines!"
"Heck I do!"
"Why're you blushin'?"
"Shut up, Butchie…I caught more fish!"
"Liar…!" – off in dash and tag…

Autumn's Evening…

It's in the sunsets now deeply golden,
the hot wind tempers down and the air
begins to share its crisp, life-giving breeze…

A lazy journey is ending, drifting here to there
to no place, musing among grassy ferns
interwoven beneath soft, billowy clouds…
From a long tousled slumber the forest awakens,
rustled by breath of the coming chill, while
fragrant meadows swell, luring worker bees
flitting flower to flower, gathering nectar…
In the distance children romp and sing in
their raucous play, eagerly chasing the
will-o-wisp…thistles lean to listen…

Angling from the trellised heights, sunbeams
scatter, dancing furtively to the low forest
floor where warm clover scents settle,
nestling to the Mother's bosom…
Nearby, the lovers' pale feet fresh from the
primrose path dally in cool waters, shattering
the pool's clarity, rippling reflections from above,
rippling Mary's image whispering, "I love…"
slowly smoothing to the coming colors…

From the leafy spires the view descends
to shrouded boughs of varying hues…glints
of gold surrendering to fire-born red,
bleeding crimson and abating greens,
all embroidered by brilliant yellows…
floating silently down, gentle as fresh-fallen
snow, carpeting the path, coloring the creek,
flowing with the current, some snagging on
branches and twigs, stenciling wavery
patterns on the pebbly creek bed…

Still others quilt the bank, dry cusps soon
flayed and broken by the spry feet of a tiny
squirrel rushing to claim his walnut grounds…
He pauses…perched motionless, as if
wondering whether to mate or gather, then
feverously resumes collecting his bounty.
Suddenly he hops to a nearby tree to stiffly
observe man's approach, ever wary…

The woodsman steps breaking the brittle tip
of a branch…he stoops down…takes it in
hand, thinking…*A bitter-sweet…Mary
loved the bitter-sweet, this one ripe in bud.
She was like the bitter-sweet, red her color,
her hair brown…and she opened
fully…sweetly… lovely…*

The sun bedding down like a purple dawn,
taking the day with it…and through the
dusk dimly seen a blackbird flutters branch
to branch…instinct leads him to others
grouping on gnarly limbs for the flight south…
Below, mushrooms tumor in muffled growth
as the blackbirds chip and clamor, anxiously
awaiting the moment…soon gathering,
rising like smoke into the air, spiraling
off and away to commence their journey…

Listen…the old she-wolf foots a lonely path
in the forest, likely heard and likely not,
sounding through the autumn…

She follows a winding trail, searching
   slumber, puts her nose to hallowed air,
   catching a whiff of past love birth and death.
   Black, growing night, the wind now colder…

     The village is shutting down…
    Lamps dim to darkness, doors close…
The spinster squeals as peals of laughter rile
   the air and little goblins scatter home
     over dry, crumpled cornhusks…
   An apple cracks, treating its tart juice to
   a freckled trickster jumping nimbly
     into bed between frosted sheets…
  Outside, a jack-o-lantern hangs wistfully
in the wind, blinking and winking till the
    the candle flickers and dies, leaving
    its hapless smile gaping to the night…

In the far woods the she-wolf howls to the
   coming moon, then trots on, stopping
     by the creek to lap the cold water…
Cold like her mate lost to summer's heat,
   lapping water alone…her cubs grown with
    mates of their own…she laps cold water…
  Then lifts her head and pricks her ears to
    the lulling drift of a mouth-harp melody,
    she approaches the clearing to listen,
    tawny fur blending with dry foxtail…

From the cabin moans an old dirge of
memory, longing, and sadness…now silence…
The woodsman lays the harp on the table and tips
his cider jug, licks the rim and sets it down,
humming low, he sings, "O Shen-an-do-ah,
I loved your daugh-ter…a-a-way you…"
His voice breaks, "Mary, oh Mary…gone…"
Drowns the wick and lies back to find his sleep,
eyes closing on the ghost image of the flame…

Staring evenly, the she-wolf, seeing the cabin
fall dark and silent, beckoned by the owl's hushed
wing, turns totting back into the trees, nose
to ground, scenting for shelter and
warmth from the coming cold…

Blue Winter Dawn…

In the wake of solemnity and icy calm,
in the dim silence where dread lays flow
at the creek water's edge, now ebbs, now
slows to a crystalline form, and the barren
ice's brazen glow, and too the sparrow
nest's abandoned gray below the
crescent moon awaits, awaits…

From the late night wells forth a storm,
looming far and nigh, as yet unborn,
from a distance beyond and coming…

In the naked woods no dancing grace,
only stark shadows still as the unclothed
dead that stand waiting…and awaiting…

Now from the distance…now it comes, the
smiting breath drops from the tine of a tall dark
oak its last leaf swirling down, and with it
snowflakes float, passing to the ground…
they as perennial tears while the leaf upon
their cushion gently settles, the last soul delivered
from the gallows…here to lie beneath a frigid
shroud, buried, hidden in dark mustiness
where damp consumes decay and
with his fellows is entombed…

Amid solemnity and icy calm the Old Mother
waves her burial on and gently nestles a golden
fawn, folding its knees to a downy death,
commending all souls and his by her sure
ceaseless breath…cast to the heaven's eternal
outlying view where night glides steadily in
ethereal drift, settling the dust of ancient
rhyme as snow upon the wooded bed, dust as
snow, as surfaced purity…as song…voiced above
and within the solemn calm where lyrical
silence awaits and blesses from afar,
blessing her song as the sky bathes
the recumbent earth with music…

Telling of ages gone, strains plucked softly
from a Grecian lyre, an evanescent flow of
nebulized flakes falling, intoning an endless
scale of millennial melody...and the trees like
tuning forks to the brumal wind moaning high and
low through bough and limb in symphonic rapture
as the ballet descends forming once again
dancing movement's grace, willowing snow
to earth while hounding winds rouse crescendos
of delight, compelling billowing waves of white,
lacing, curtaining from earth to sky...

The Old Mother leads the burial on, interring
dear ones in the dark, blanketing each in
white, turning cold to warm...the lyre golden,
the fawn lies frozen, is all and is nothing...

Hush...hush now and listen...
Her song sings yet another verse as the
she-wolf foots the snow, wearily tasting its kind
depth, wanting, sensing, black warm all...and finds a
place beneath the oak where the last leaf lies, then
slowly folds, her body bedded in the snow...

The wind combs the grizzled fur and lifts
her aggrieved soul through the trees,
joining her spirit to the fawn's...
A rude gust bears the vision to the
woodsman's dream...haunted
each night by the wolf-head cloud...

Hearing a death cry, he wakes to listen, sets
his feet to the cold wood floor and pulls the
patch quilt about his shoulders. Frail breath
fogs the air as he stares evenly, eyes intent
on the golden haze glowing from the fire,
black-red embers softly flamed, casting
dire shadows on the walls and ceiling...
The woodsman stares evenly recalling a
griefful night in a gone winter when
the shadows danced the very same...

...Been sitting up with Mary a fortnight now,
over the past four days she has not awakened,
we have no way of knowing her end...
Doc Griffith says there's nothing to be done,
except ease her pain and comfort her...

Falling asleep, it's late night when I wake,
I look to Mary...her eyes open, watching me...
Spurred by hope I kneel to her...but only her eyes
are alive, her lips and skin, deathly pale and chalky...
But her eyes...Mary's eyes tear like a young girl,
her heart beating in throe of love...her lips quiver,
and seeing her wish to speak I lean my ear to her,
my eyes to her, listening to her faint breath...

"Daniel, please go...no, you must..."

Hours seem to pass as I grip her hand,
pleading to her eyes, pleading, "No..."
But she speaks again only this time weaker...

*"Daniel, I gave you my love...my life...
this we cannot share..."*

*I shake my head and cannot speak, cannot
swallow...griped by fear tightening my throat...
Now she is the one pleading with all her strength...*

*"Please...Daniel...leave me now...this we
must do alone...always believed...never
knew when...Daniel...?"*

*I turn from her side and walk away,
crying bitter tears to myself,
and never speak to her again...*

The woodsman sits at the edge of the bed,
staring evenly, eyes on the golden glow,
sits in his cabin, empty cabin, all alone,
thinking what was left unsaid...
"I love you, Mary...love you..."

Longing for her warmth, he walks to the fire,
grasps the wrought-iron poker and stirs the
ashes, granting air, gaining heat...then tosses a
split of hickory on the coals, sparks trailing
up the chimney, flames in hiss and roar,
coiling and snapping at the wood...

He lingers for a time then walks to the window and
stands, eyes intent, his warm breath melting frost
on the pane, soon clearing to the view outside…
He admires the snow…its purity and essence,
remembering youth and play, carols, candles,
and mysteries sung…remembering days skating
and frisking…and the nights…first and always
remembering Mary…finally he lowers his
head, turns from the scene and shuffles
back to bed…to sleep and forget…

Leaving the woodsman's side, his cabin hedged with
snow, cabin darkly alone…slipping away, away
through the sylvan scene lain to peace by the
Old Mother's wand…in long white gowns her
sylphs skip dancing over wood and creek in
trailing glow, sprinkling glints of the astral sky,
imbuing this wonderland with air freshly
sweet as watermelon split open and shared…

And the Old Mother runs spitting vital juices,
casting new seeds to nourish the bones below,
breathing warmth to the dark consuming decay
to conceive next spring's embryos…dancing
on through the burial till she comes to the
she-wolf frozen, bows to her fond dead
in appeal to the surrounding wind to
receive the she-wolf's soul…then
bids the she-wolf peaceful sleep…

Suddenly the Old Mother leaves,
and now the view bodes sullen...
the trees abruptly stand like stark intruders
offering grim similitudes...hands risen from graves,
held stiff to the air, begging for help, reaching,
hands frozen in grasp of soldier lads
whose brothers felled them there...

Only briefly is there peace...but also beauty
in brooding starkness as there is life in death
and motion in stillness, for what is coming is yet
to be...borne from distance beyond and coming.
Who knows what's to come? Perhaps a feral grace?
Is not the she-wolf enhanced by tinseled fur?
Her coat once gray and bristled, now winter pure?
Seeing her prone beneath the oak, she sheens,
silvery kin to the Golden Fleece...

Now turn from the nightscape etched black
and white to the pearly promise mirrored in the
land's broad robe...trees sheathed in icy glaze,
viewing as did the woodsman this solemn night,
turning from sad memory to the window,
gazing on stars aglitter near and far,
luminous off the crusted snow...
Viewing as the woodsman viewed radiance,
grasping a pristine flake, holding it to a light,
a candle's living flame...and through this prism
a flood of color unfolds spiraling patterns before

and within his eyes, beholding a kaleidoscopic
gyre spun from one geometric mote to
form a rainbow of music color life…

Behold the woodsman at his window,
viewing a blue winter dawn of music color life,
remembering with the woodsman…play and
youth, remembering the days skating and
frisking, and the nights…remembering Mary.
Now walk with the woodsman as he shuffles,
walk him back to bed, to sleep and forget…

A rabbit runs freely dancing over the snow,
basking in the radiance of a blue winter dawn
near the woodman's cabin…darkly alone…
wherein he sleeps and always believed but never
knew…wherein he awakes to know
he'll breathe good air no more…

"And without the world of gone and dead
we are voices humming the shadow's sigh,
the quiet breeze which breeds the seed…
whispering to the flower to bloom,
to the heart to love, and when to cease,
feathering to owl wing and wind,
softly quilled to a silence fore and aft
of all that moves and plays…"

The Cedar by Karl Ramberg

WIND CRY

The old men say,
Earth only endures.
Ye spake truly,
Ye spake well... – death song of the Teton Sioux

Long since was the Summer,
The heat raged in flood,
Bereaving the Earth of living breath,
Leaving her rivers dry.
Then Autumn blustered arrogant and full,
Threatening sundry foes
As the wind and the eagle vie.
Soon would come Spring when all renews,
The coyote relinquishing its prey
To hunt a mate.
But now the Earth was ice,
The lone cedar twisting before the wind
With Winter upon the land.

The first rays of dawn tipped the horizon
And sun-dewed over the snow,
Rustling the prairie from its cold silence.
And only the cry of the hawk could be heard
Beneath the still, gray sky.
Then faint as a moving shadow
Came a figure from the fading night,
Man-strides of dogged length,
Scuffing grass and snow.

A week before blizzard winds had rifled the plains,
Leaving sullen drifts in the lingering thaw.
The man paused and held his palm to the dawn.
He was young, his eyes like flint,
Dark and piercing as one seeking prey.
He breathed heavily,
His nostrils hungry to drink the air,
For he had run far to reach this spot by dawn.
He stood on the brow of a rolling hill facing east,
Catching the first rays of the rising sun.
Around him span the "Rim of the World,
"Wherein walk the Four Winds…
"Man's Abode," said the old men.

Keen to ancient fidelity
He removed his shirt,
Baring his chest to the living sun,
Fortifying his body to endure privation
While his soul made prayer.
And removed too his hard boots
As not to harm the Mother's bosom,
But like a soft rain, warm and of the flesh.

He took the red kerchief
Which soaked his sweat working the fields
And tied a bandana around his hair.
Thus he stood as the sun rose high,
Till his ruddy skin warmed and darkened,
Till his angular cheekbones shadowed,
Till his faded Levis grew taut against his thighs.

Then kneeling to his grandfather's calumet,
He took its crimson stem in hand,
Reverent of its color and its fateful flame.
The calumet, trimmed with feathers of the Lark,
The peace pipe, more precious than a warrior's lance.

He filled the bowl with tobacco from a cigarette
And stood, proud and embolden,
Like a man often stands before an old god.

The wind had blown and the wind had ceased.
And from the eastern nadir the man raised his head,
Offering smoke to the zenith:

> *O Wakonda! Great Spirit Wind!*
> *Creator of my breath!*
> *Receive my breath into thine*
> *As the sky receives the bird…*
> *Soon! For my life is feeble!*
> *My spirit is offered*
> *That my prayer be answered…*

Then to the sun:

> *May ye shine long*
> *That my body grows warm and strengthens,*
> *That my prayer be of beauty and greatness*
> *As my sorrow is great…*

And to the Earth he whispered:

Take my words as many seeds unto thy bosom.
May my tongue be as truthful as thou art fertile,
That my prayer be worthy and of substance...

Continuing the sacrament, he smoked
To the Four Quarters: to the North,
Where the winds blew cold in winter;
To the South, where vital warmth
And fresh rains fostered;
To the East, where the sun rose,
And to the West, where the sun set,
That his breath be as their breath,
That he be in harmony with his abode.

A tumble-weed stirred.
A rabbit's fallow fur lay torn.
The man's breath bore the wind anew,
Spurring his trance,
Wooing unto his worship.
It spread his arms to alar form and passed.
His eyes closed before a cloud,
And as a tender root will part the rock
His spirit escaped his flesh
And untethered soared aloft,
Screaming, crying,
As the eagle first cleaves the air:

O Wakonda!
Man is of the Sky!
Woman of the Earth!
My courage has withered and I am cowed
As her fruit is bruised and laid to spoil.
Am I ungrateful…angry…?
I stand outcast, a stranger in my home!

A lone wolf I thought I was.
I roamed in many places
And set my foot down many paths.
Not one dropped of fatness!
I am weary, O Wakonda!
I am weary…"

Wakonda neared,
The wind His witness,
Blowing the man's hair straight back.
The man dreamed…
And dreamt he flew within the clouds
And the clouds were black
And the Sky a deep purple
And the sun a tarnished rose
And his body was made of stone.
All this Wakonda allowed him view
That he should learn there is no permanence
Save the granite, cold and gray.
The man feared the vision.
He ran and fell.

He reached for succor but there was none.
At last he gave sup
In hope of dim memories:

> O Wakonda!
> I must pray to you,
> For I want to live on this land.
> But my heart is bitter, O Father,
> For the land is my home no longer.
> Ruin is my home,
> And rubble,
> Black, cold, and hollow is my home...
>
> O Wakonda!
> I went to hunt the buffalo;
> I found their bones.
> And the big grass and little grass
> On which they grazed for centuries
> Was plowed and put to seed.
> Millions dead made the furrows fertile.
> And too I sought the fragrant pasque
> Where it had always bloomed,
> But the meadows were pastured by cattle
> And rarely its sacred scent I find upon the land...
>
> O Wakonda!
> Shall I tell you it is harsh, cruel?
> That the season's song now seems a dirge?
> Shall I tell you it has been long
> Since I caressed a woman as I should...?

Her nipple is like a bead of rain
And one must take her tenderly.
Yet when I grip she writhes and screams.
I give no love, I give her pain...

O Wakonda, I pray thee!
I ask for little.
O Father, I pray thee!
I ask for naught
Save for the music as from a war drum pounds...

Divest of all joy,
Dweller of lone dirt roads,
He had picked tobacco and drilled for oil
Till his auburn skin blistered.
Divest of all joy,
He retained only his pride,
Vestige of an austere legacy.
Once he traveled to a city
And stepped into a bar and
To rude caress gave war cry
As he knifed the man's fat belly
And left him bleeding on the floor.

In the long silence
Sweat iced upon his brow.
He feared the Spirit wind would give no answer,
And as request more aptly comes
To a child that cries,
He wept before his Father.
In true humility he uttered to his Father:

O Wakonda!
Please hear me...
I come a beggar.
I am a man no longer.
I am lost even to myself.
Like a dog without a master
I run astray.
Please!
Tell me what I am
That I may be a man again.

O Wakonda, I beg thee!
I ask for little.
O Father, I pray thee!
I ask for naught
Save for the music as from a war drum sounds...

To this the Spirit wind listened.
To this the Great wind gave answer.
Through the undulating vastness
Wakonda waved His hand...

Lo! The prairie, of wide immensity and sky,
Procurer of desire, harbinger of fate,
Of emerald waters and azure horizon,
Land of cherished myth and lore.
Solitary within its bounds he stood.
From afar...of a distance beyond view
Even to an eagle's eye,
A whirlwind was born and still another
And died and was reborn.

Verily they numbered as raindrops upon the prairie,
Heralding the Spirit's coming,
Soon converging unto his trance.

Now the air lay low and calm,
Now the wind awoke and howled
Like ghosts of wolves pursuing
Buffalo thundering down.
The whirlwind closed around,
Enveloping his rigid form
Then heft him skyward,
Swooning through a mystic realm
Of fluid darkness and fiery visions.
Within this mind cave he listened
to the flush rhythm of his close heartbeat.

A whisper came from yonder
Like the Corn Maiden's gentle sigh
Breathing over the snow,
Beckoning him, "Please draw closer,
Fear not, child, please draw nigh."
As a breath over dry and yellow cornhusks,
Urging, "Come forward, forward, come…"

Now in the grasp of true divinity
Wakonda's mighty thunder
Caught and pitched him through hail and levin,
Through black unfathomed heavens
Then lowered him like gentle rain

Amid surrounding darkness
Beside a blazing fire
Where war drums were resounding
With music of the warrior
And fond rhythms of the plains...

The vision faded and all was silent.
He opened his eyes to the hillside.
Before him stretched the barren prairie,
The grasses brown where there was no snow.
Winter was yet.
He saw the day, the sun slanting west.
His body felt empty, cold.
He gazed upon the Sky, the Earth,
And over the Four Quarters,
And stood defeated, deposed,
Throughout the vast panorama
He saw no remnant of his lineage.

In vain gesture fraught with rage,
Lack of option and broken promise,
He griped his anguish in calloused hands,
Snarling through his tears:

> *Wakonda is like the great white virgin*
> *Who offered me her beauty.*
> *At my approach she veiled her face*
> *And bade me follow through the night,*
> *Uttering softly of her love the while:*
> *"Faith," said she, "I offer love eternal."*

When I pressed my hands in need
She turned to marble stone.

Wakonda tells me, "You are hungry, child?
"Here are sweet odors. Be satisfied!"
That stone I pounded into dust,
I ask Wakonda, "How…?"
How does one live in a joyless home?
Be satisfied?
Hunger is cruel and painful, yes!
Though it can be endured,
And I have known hunger.
But this emptiness in my heart
Is more than hunger.
This ache I cannot endure…

Sorrow gave way to despair,
Having vent his rage on the Sacred,
Like the flight of an unfledged arrow
The man trembled uncertain.
He clasped his arms to his shoulders
And swayed from side to side
In question whether to live or die.
Nature's shrewdest number is the dual,
To love or hate, to kill or no.
The man who laughs more often cries.
One will swear the truth
To cloud a lie.
Mercy is the only measure.
The wind breathed over him,
"Abide, sad child, abide…"

He thought of his mother,
Recalling her dear old voice,
Felt her cradle his head
As mothers will,
"Abide, sad child, abide…"

He unclasped his shoulders
And hung his head in shame
And pity of himself
And wept before his Father:

    Forgive me, O Wakonda!
    Forgive your orphan.
    I am lost, I have no parents, no home…

    O Wakonda!
    Tell me of my home
    That I may know my home if I see it…

A virile wind buffeted the hillside,
Whistling over its wizened brow,
Frightening the man as his Father's reprimand…

    Father have pity on me!
    Father, I am crying in thirst!
    There is nothing here to sate me!

    When I sat beside the warriors' fire

For one grass-blade moment
I knew the old men's tale all told.
Now I know nothing!
Nor even a scent I smell!

O Wakonda!
Tell me of my past
That I may at least dream…

The hillside clothed in shadow
As Wakonda reached forth His hand
And bade the man to kneel,
Then stirred the dust
And formed a cloud before him,
Then waved His hand and passed…

From the cloud stepped a Warrior,
Stepped a proud majestic Warrior.
His robe was crimson, blue, and yellow.
His face was chiseled deep and raw.
He viewed the prairie like an eagle,
His eyes set to the hills afar,
Gazed through distance into time.

The Warrior spoke, his words solemn,
In a voice that echoed thunder.
He spoke to one man as to many,
Spake he pure as brave Tecumseh,
His words and bearing of revered age…

Abide, sad child, abide.
The old men's tale is unfolding,
The old men's tale will be told…

In the beginning all was stillness.
The moon was not, nor the stars, nor the sky.
All was darkness, there was nothing.
Then motion swept forth and truly
The very surge and beating of the sea was born.
Lightning flashed and the broad face of Heaven
Shone over the waters and valleys of the Earth.
A subtle breath set the pinion of the sparrow.
Behold! All was born!
Save for man.

This is the saga primeval I speak,
Of the sun whose blessed rays
So colored the Earth's embosomed life
And shaded dark from night to day,
Thus bestowing time…
Of the way of the winds,
Of the forces that patterned the seasons
And with the first Spring bestowed
The vital procreative seed of nature.
Of man I speak, of his first coming
And all the ages to follow…

Mother Corn roamed the Earth,
Father moved through the Heavens,
As yet there were no children.
Mother Corn had a yearning.

She tore bits of her heart
And planted seeds of maize,
Sacred kernels to nourish
The flesh of man to his creation.
Her labors finished, she spoke:
'This corn is my heart,
And it shall be to my children
As milk from my breast.'

Though the seeds were sown
The Mother could not be fertile
Except by will of the Father.
And so it was that even while
Her fruit lay dormant
Father wet the soil with resinous rain
And thus was man conceived.
In the mist of the morning he arose,
And the leaves and grasses stirred.

Man stood before the broad waters,
Before the precipice of the sea,
Then turned and journeyed westward
And became a denizen of the land,
North, South, East, and West lands,
Preyed on the fauna and basked in the sun.

Man's dominion was of grandeur,
Such abundance as never was.
Deer were plenty on the mountains.
Elk and buffalo roamed the plains.

There were waters fresh and flowing,
Forever flowing! Forever flowing!
Rivers too numerous to be named.
Streams and lakes swarmed with fishes,
Trout and salmon teemed,
Overhead trilled larks and swallows.
Trees and skies festooned with game,
Fowl were turkey, quail, and prairie hen,
Their meat was juicy! All were sweet!
There were marshes lush and supple
Where ducks and geese fed in the reeds,
While the water-moccasin slipped
Quietly beneath the cypress
And through the mossy green.

The giant redwood and sequoia,
Dueling each towards the sky,
Housed the eagle and the grizzly.
Tall and stout-limbed stood the alder,
Quaking aspen, fir, spruce, and pine.
Oak and hickory grew on uplands,
Red maple and elm in the low,
Willow and sycamore along the streams.
There thrived in forest and woodland
Raccoon, possum, woodchuck, and fox.
The bear dipped honey from old tree hollows,
The beaver mudded his dam and cave.
Through shade and niche preyed the puma,
The coyote, wolverine, and the marten.
All was wilderness! All untamed!
Truly man's dominion was abundant,

No less in breadth than beatitude.
From primal dawn he stood in awe
Of wonders worn through the seasons.
Was it not Spring's sweet breath
That chased Winter from the land
And set the laurel flower blooming?
Maiden petals of such beauty
As to clothe a maiden's breasts...
Phlox in raiment dressed the hillsides,
In rich cluster blessed the springs
Where warm breezes caught
And kissed their velvet freshness.

And Ho! Summers were resplendent!
Humming bees roamed the meadows
Searching their golden nectar
Above sweet clover in the grass.
Lo! The summers too were pale...
The lone cedar stood upon the prairie
Wreathed in dust, unyielding,
Symbol of endurance,
Sentinel of the drought,
While dry grasses awaited thunder
Of bison bull, cow and calf.

Ah! Autumn's crisp and soothing sunlight
Endowed the Earth's serenity,
Turned maples to flame among the conifers
And sent birds migrating south.
O Winters of starvation! O Winters of ordeal!
Were it not for the pure snowfall

Which lay virgin all the land
Life would have been dire.
For from a blizzard stepped
The White Buffalo who bade man
To have faith in Wakonda,
Bade man give worship,
And left man the calumet...

O seasons rare!
All were beauteous! All were fair!

Herein, my son, your fathers dwelled,
Roamed and hunted in profuse.
All the land from peak to prairie,
All the land, the woods and hills,
All the land was the Redman's.
O my child! This was our home!
Long the haunt of the Redman,
Long before the white man came
With pox, ax, firewater, and bullets
And set the Iron Horse upon the land.
Yea, long before the white man
Brought his pestilence to our home,
O my child! It was Nature's palace!
Her palace pristine...sublime.
Vast deep forests flourished,
Winds were redolent and moist.
The prairie stretched on forever,
Offering bounteous life to the Indian...

Told in the rich fruits of the Mesa Verde!
Told in the mystic agony of the Sun Dance!
Told in the ordeal of our very existence!
So harsh each trial and adversity,
So utter the Indian's reign.

Sioux, Cheyenne, and Dakota,
Comanche, Osage, and Omaha,
Pawnee, Apache, Fox, and Blackfoot,
Hopi, Crow, and Navajo,
All were warriors of great stamina!
All proclaimed domains and grounds!
Built their earth lodge and their teepee,
Wickiup, wigwam, and pueblo,
Where they bade their lives would follow!
Where they bade their sons would grow!

Ah! Dear mornings of tranquility...
The sun rose over the village,
Smoke curled up from the hogans
As children romped about the fires,
Romped to warm their hungry bellies
And gain sweet meat from their mothers.
Mornings made for play and pleasure.
They learned to run and hunt and swim,
Mimic birdsong and the coyote's call.
All the mysteries of the forest!
All curiosities they beheld!
They viewed the nestlings
Of the horned owl hatching,

Plucked quills from the porcupine.
Great the wonders! Great the mysteries!
And great would be their wisdom
Once age had run its rhyme.
But as they grew to man and woman
Then! The time of test and courage
Then! The days of life's travail.
Courage for the brave and warrior,
Fertility for the maiden and her labor
All would strive! All would suffer!
Countless trials would ensue!

When a maiden's breasts had ripened
Beneath her hair, long and silken,
Hair that outshone the raven's wing,
Yea! When a maiden's fruit proved ready,
The young braves vied for her favor,
And feats of valor were the order,
Judged they by counting coup!
And he who rode his pony swiftly
Over the rippling sea of grass,
And like the wolf was most cunning
And generous in hunt and battle,
And dropped much fatness on his path,
He would win the maiden's hand.
Then all the tribe would gather
In witness to their promise
To share their flesh and Mother Earth
Till the last bird circled from the sky.
Their nuptial dance and feast surfeit,

*They escaped to a hidden grove
And loved among the violets
And lilies of the hillside…
They slept, their dreams were hopeful.
They woke and gave thanks to Wakonda,
Knelt before Grandmother Cedar
And prayed for many children.
Together they would carry forth,
Plant their crops in wholesome soil,
Harvest pumpkin, squash, corn, potato
To store with meat, fruit, nuts, and honey,
For there were many children.
So they carried forth in joy and want,
The warrior and his squaw,
Till they huddled with the aged,
Gnawed and bent by winter's tines,
Each memory consumed as by a fire,
Scenting for death in the quiet evenings,
Evenings of solemnity
When the sun set red and calm.*

*Such was the cycle from birth to death,
Though tribe to tribe were many and varied,
And fierce and strange one to the other,
Much was the same, all unending.
Till night fell and all ended!
O my child! All was lost!*

One day the sun rose on our people,
The next it set.
The white man stormed ashore,
Despoiled hunting ground and garden,
Seizing all our lands.
Through peril of promise
Beset and starved us to submission,
Chained us like dogs
And made us sit beside his fire.
Was ever man so ill-done?
So diminished in heart and soul?
We had no choice! We had to fight!
Man's pride will not suffer him to grovel!

Need I tell all that followed?
It was a desperate struggle certain,
Though at times a noble one…
True, Red Cloud won a victory,
He cleared the Bozeman Trail of whites.
And great Gall under Sitting Bull
Wiped foul Custer from our lands…
The Little Bighorn was our pleasure.
Dull Knife and Little Wolf
Led the Cheyenne to their homes.
But what of all the others? What befell them?
What of Satanta, tempestuous Kiowa chief,
Who spat upon his capture,
'I don't want to settle!
I love to roam the prairie!
These soldiers cut the timber!

They kill the buffalo!
When I see that it feels as if
My heart would burst with sorrow!'
He jumped to his death from a prison window.
And Satank, also a Kiowa chief,
Who bitterly cried, 'I am no child!'
Then did the same.
And Black Kettle, Cheyenne chief,
Who ran from his lodge, white flag raised,
While Colonel Chivington slaughtered
Women and children at Sand Creek.
O gallant soldiers! Ye Colorado Volunteers!
What of Captain Jack and Scareface Charlie?
Both courageous Modoc warriors!
Both were hanged for doing battle!
Both were fighting for their homes!
Finally with Wounded Knee
Their execution was complete,
The Sioux chief Bigfoot lay slain,
Struggling to rise, frozen in the snow.

Whatever was left of our former glory
Was mere memory, forever lost.
In those final years arose
The flailing hopes of a dying people.
Wovoka became our prophet
And bade the children of Wakonda
Dance! And all shall be restored to you!
For five days the people would fast and dance,
But all would worsen.

*The Ghost Dance died with Bigfoot
And three hundred Sioux at Wounded Knee.*

*O my child! One day the sun rose, then it set!
There is the tale in words I have spoken,
The old men's tale has been told...*

The man sat slumped and weary
Before the vanquished warrior.
The sky darkened, the wind blew cold.
The warrior spirit vanished, a shadow in the dusk.
At last the man stood and guessed his fate...

*What is there to be done?
O Wakonda! What?
I cannot live their life,
In the words of Smohalla, I cannot!*

'They ask me to plow the ground.
Shall I take a knife and tear my Mother's bosom?
Then when I die
She will not take me to Her breast.

'They ask me to dig for stone.
Shall I dig under Her skin for Her bones?
Then when I die
I cannot enter Her body to be born again.
'And they ask me to cut the grass
And make hay and sell it
And be rich like they.

But how can I cut my Mother's hair?'
They are shameless people.
I cannot accept their evil ways.
But what is there to be done?
O Wakonda! Forget this child!
I shall not ask you for the old life,
I am not yet a fool…

The man drew on his boots and shirt,
Turned and faded into the dusk.
The wind soon covered his tracks
And the peace pipe, left fallen in the snow.

"Sky and Earth are everlasting!
Old age is a thing of evil!
Charge!" – Wants To Die, Dakota Warrior

Face to Face by Karl Ramberg

DEATH PSALM

Lamp of life, in the last flicker of my moment
I leave the house of shared dreams. My body the
walls, my eyes the windows, the season is winter.
Frost chills each surface, indifferent to life,
this gone flesh. These chinks and crannies rot
through, the panes crack. The decay complete
once I'm skull and all time and presence is equal.
From the Ruins of Angkor to a creek-cleft in Kansas,
this hand, this dust…as all images, thoughts,
dreams, pains, and pleasures disperse,
extinguished, flue and flame ceased…

Beyond a certain point all becomes memory,
we memory's child, nourished of cascading scenes,
the seeming chimera of diverse nebula, driftwood of
the seven seas…brittle and skeletal as kindling for
a sea-god's pyre. Death, immutable as the tides,
her palsy flames consume till singly we yield,
life a mute curse, a forgotten utterance.
We, the only copy extant, are burned,
our spirits decanted from the flesh,
drawn to the depths of a bedless sea…

So the old man picks an apple as the
little boy rubs morning dew from his eyes.
With his knife the old man begins peeling
the skin, each slice revealing a further
verse in faint illumination like

fireflies in a starlit archipelago…
Amid a collage of vagrant forms evolves
visions of my hands at their anointed tasks.
In a verdant copse as a child I picked berries
from nettled vines…the fruit let to ferment
in jugs of clay so that with age I could
better taste my cellared sorrow…

Wheat when ripe and flaxen I reaped in
fulsome swaths from fertile fields, the wind-
flailed grain borne in baskets of woven reeds
and stored on mats of cushioned straw…
We labored in trust, each endowed, our harvest
milled into flour. Hopeful, sharing feast and hunger,
arduous bondage between stomach and hand
till selfish appeal infested our hearts and
envy and enmity railed…then came
rage, violence, and devastation…

Wandering lost, our weary spirits converged
on a just voice calling a council of elders to
restore the pattern of our tribal soul…in thirst
for guidance, even temperament and purpose,
the trail of assiduous peace, faring over
perilous reefs to reach kinder shores.
Yeast for text, dough for sacrament, our
sacred nave an oven whose blessed heat
bestowed odors of clover and hay-mowing,
the glassy dew of morning pastures, the thunder's
brassy laughter, and far tonings laced in snowflakes,
while our hands broke bread to savor the gift of
kinship molded in the brown-baked crust,

and therein, the nascent meat of love…
Pressing flint to clay, my hands etched rifts
of lambent forms entombed in hieroglyphs.
There, I absorbed the mystic emanations of the
Milky Way into my palms, prepared to rise
and take the arena opposite Orion…
There, I loved through the boundless night on
a celestial carpet, caressed woman's beauty
and sought her supple depth…she, as
ineffably conceived as the Universe…

My hands have folded beneath clouds of
despair, cupped to the warmth of my breath
like doves hunched under awnings
from the cold December rains…

So many days-seasons-years my hands
have blistered like tattoos livid on my skin,
so many ways I've gripped and drove against
the earth…this shovel of my pain…

When young, its handle coarse and roughly
hewn, through many sun-soaked labors my bloody
palms stained the grain, through years of shouldered
burden my callused hands sanded smooth its scars,
many a curse I vowed to lacquer shut its pores.
This shovel once thrust so doggedly in task and toil,
its handle polished like ivory or an ancient bone
which over eons attains the divinity of marble.
This lowly cudgel, this unlit torch, we bequeath to
another, with pious utterance relay the stave
hand to hand, like runners in endless quest…

When at last I relinquish my burden in sigh
to my mortal crib and fade from my beloved, her
far, far shadow…in death my hands will crimp,
fissure and blacken like broken slate, their
presence frightful, their touch odious, abhorrent,
as the rotting dead are ever the pariah of life…

Close by, the little boy laps like a bobber
to the sage cadence of the old man's words,
savoring another slice of the proffered apple…
The child looks to its hands, intent, curious how
they've dirtied that day, yet hardly aged, then
looks to the old man's hands, leathery and
dappled by dark pigment common to men
who spend their lives in sun-blessed orchards…

They look to one another, boy to man, oddly
mirrored, joint…and I the same, soon their ghost.
An apple shared in apt catharsis for what awaits…

I put a penny in, good for one more grain of
time it seems, and will pace the pavement of an
anonymous city, stones laid out like pale corpses
beneath the night's crape ceiling. I journey
with three magi: a beggar, a shepherd, a thief,
each in want of faith, woman, and home, all
lost along the diagonal bridging birth to death.
A grave heat, dense, like a dark intimation, weighs
down, oppressing the weary pilgrim as all are bled,
nor even the virgin's seminal flower let to breathe.

Resignation imbues the spirit, indifferent, deaf to
plaintive cries and pleas as the high priest extols
his devotees for their reverence and piety,
praising each hymnal curse and agony,
blessing the fool masses cowed at his feet.
Lo, he is death…his ritual replete, unending…

I see there is no sanctity and walk on, passing
through hiatus and time to enter antiquity's musty
realm where my will abates, lame, evanescent, mixed
with rank humors and disquiet shades in Aegean
catacombs…I find no simulacra of Helen, only
the mournful roll of the tides and the briny
depths the fathomless sea has wept for her…

Borne on a black wind webbed to the sky,
carried over millennia of upheaval, I view the
earth's vast transient topography, her gardens
in ruin, her fields desolate…then to my grave.

At the wrought-iron gate rigor mortis and decay
already set in, the frame twists on its hinge, rusted,
frozen ajar. Already the bronze lettering of my stone
corrodes accursed green…while spidery grapnels
detain each with the silent tenacity of cobwebs
that acquiesce in shadow till only stillness is afoot.
Moments pass, days or more, perhaps seasons…

Presently, the gaunt rider posting the burial
carriage dismounts — a tragic old form, frail and
menial, steps forth, his eyes dimmed by cataracts

which cause him endless myopia and pain.
Hatless, hair grizzled, unshorn, from his shoulders
hangs a woolen cape, its satin collar frayed and
worn, a futile weave against the bloodless chill.
Sackcloth binds his feet in the manner of a slave,
hands large and gnarled like unearthed legumes,
and whether I glance to his left or his right,
at his back looms a dusky, trackless void…

I greet him, the old doorman, his posture
straightens slightly, his voice rusty from long
disuse as he rasps his question, not wholly
exempt from words: "Is it so necessary,
really…that life be preferred to death…?
I answer "Yes" – which he accepts in mute
deferral. Then I ask for a brief reprieve…which
again he grants with the dry apathy of the dead…

I gaze once more upon fire, food, and friends
then to the revolving panorama, and like a pebble
cast to a lake's calm surface, my vision ripples forth
seeking the contour and substance of my life.
But ask answer of immutable stone, choose
whatever rock you think abiding, once
thrown it will vanish into the sea…
In the woods I walk under arched trees
dripping night fumes, vile and venomous.
Wolves howl, taunting from the shadows…
I pause, breathless before their baleful pant
as they circle in mock, scenting my trail.

A blue jay shrieks and bids me go faster...
In feint and weave, crouching, running to escape,
I struggle against tangled briars in hope to meld with
the woods, a supple, elusive shadow, yet still a flame,
luminous to my yellow-eyed pursuers...
"You devils!" I curse, frantic, in desperate flight.
Through interstices of panic, vague intimations,
more intuited than thought, pervade my being,
an incomprehensible déjà vu claims my will.

No longer pursued, metamorphosed, now a
wolf...newly acquired member of the pack...
A savage presence bristles along my spine in one
elongated fusion, I am my own precursor, delirious
and instinctual, keenly feral senses welling forth.
The air yields to my primal howl, again transformed,
now the lead wolf of lusty urge racing through
the night like rowdy laughter through a bar...

Hunger sated, once fed, forsaken...an incipient
quiescence returns self to form, to prior flesh and
vernacular in witness of an impending cataclysm.
I, mortal numen, harken to the valley of primeval
germination, where dwelt the determinant seed in
fertile splendor. Adorned by succulent flora, the
very grasses in luster provoked passion and rut.
Pronghorn, buffalo, and other ruminants ranged
through humid night to arid dawn in multitudes
beneath auroral skies on through the horizon,
following to the setting sun, the last light filtering

from fuchsia clouds scintillating off a narrow river
twining through the broad alluvial plain,
each swale and contour lush and fertile.
The valley which in rainy season legend claimed
flooded bluff to bluff, the waters soon wafting
blue to green over the somnolent seas of grass…
A pristine morning, the valley sleeps unaware an
incubus forms and prepares to mount a thunderous
storm, thrusting his lightning to her loamy thighs.
Incantations of dim origin wake the river's
savage soul…at first a low rumbling like kettle
drums rising through the valley far as eye
or ear perceive, a disturbing prelude
as a songbird braves the looming silence…

Presently a wall of water, a vast dark phalanx,
ushers forth a day of ruin…the brute, numb to
piteous plea, deaf and blind, a voluminous mass
bulling over trees like rampant hordes of
yowling horsemen, raging waters roiling down,
seizing all the valley as she submits to ravage…

The flood rises in waves, smothering untold
lives in its turbid wake…climaxing, subsiding,
ending in woeful hush as the valley lies prone,
her wounds untended, her cries gone silent…
All this before a century of iron plows make
her yield utterly, dust-blown and scarred
with stretch marks on her bosom…

Something calls, vague, insistent – not the
old grave-keep passing on, but a revenant urge
summoned by the dawn's arrival upon the night.
So the subliminal subverts the mind, I turn as
the flood recedes before a mildly pungent breeze,
then pearly droplets grace the flesh, sensually
soothing as if bathed by the ocean's balm...
Valley mists hang in ethereal suspension,
opaline, spectral, slowly rising in vaporous
filament to the eastern sky while sunlight
tinsels down enlivening each color...

Again I turn, unknowing of where or why,
my body numb, drained of all labor and fatigue.
My hands, reverting to dust, relinquish their hold
on bone and scythe, nor grasp nor reap no more.
An aborning ghost come to a forked road, and
which path taken matters not, both narrow
and rutted, overgrown with weeds.
Wading stale waters, I inhale musky vapors
of decay, oblivious, weaving forth, a witless clown,
in echo after echo, beyond an irrevocable boundary,
shedding my mortal skin, leaving the vibrant
corporeal maze for the dayless, dreamless,
nightless, nameless, now nearly consummate...

Hushed in view of a mansion, as one escaped
and hunted, the entire environ and its terrain
incomprehensible, resigned to whatever path
the inevitable may offer, whatever judgment
or blind omnipotence attends my cryptic fate,

a last gasp… like a shadow relieved of substance.
As surely as the flesh yields to lye, sweet-plucked
strains yield a sigh, then yields once more,
drifting, seized by a far tenuous wailing,
the melody, an old hymn, fades and
yields to a static silence boding death…

In view of this mansion, a home I have known
and loved, and loved within, its many windows of
uneven glaze and number by nature predestined
as all human traits and contrarieties to be
continually reborn, resolved, and torn asunder.
Enwalled in my cherished home I stand before a
mirror reflecting each moment as all obscurities
are stripped away before a raw, naked clarity
revealing every interstice and rhythm, and I see
that the mansion stands in reflection of its skeletal
ruin across the way…as if the road were the
medium that bore the traffic of vacuous truth,
like vanished footprints trailing bygone flesh…
The mirror's quicksilver surface, transient as an
early frost, begins to thaw, self-fragments devolving
to dreg certitude held in the humus of my heart…

The sun's torrid sting bleeds like salt in a wound,
savoring the stink of death as paint flecks and fades,
shingles loosen and rot, and my woolen clothes fray
to rags, my flesh to ashes. Before the pitiless wind
rafters weaken, cornices sag, lintels fall, while
its icy claws reach to bone and marrow…

The pillars which have sustained the awning now
accede to bullying time…the porch collapses.
So too the lifelines on my brow and hands,
the remembrance of intimacies and caresses,
of evenings cocooned in fond talk with
whiskey flasks and joyful faces, all are erased…

Updrafts swirl, subterranean worms in vie for
entry, seeking passage through chinks and crannies,
while sere heat and cold shatter panes that on former
mornings held dewdrops clung to outer walls, now
seeping to the inner walls as well. And likewise,
tears that soothed both sight and pain, dear springs
that wet my weary eyes, cease to flow, my vision
a desert, brittle as worms cast to the hot sun.
A dark wind howls through hollow sockets and
and halls, stripping the walls in chaotic pattern as
clusters of thought fall like leaves in vertiginous
spin to the flames, all crimpling to ember
and smoke and everlasting futility…

The road dispels, the mirror too, as images
merge, disrobed and sated. On the ground, next
to me, lying twisted as an oak limb, my skeleton.
And beyond, my former home, more forbidding
than a grave, a beckoning presence that defies
and tempts you to enter its dark cavity…
At once deposed, absolved, and absorbed
in swift infinitesimal measure, nor one
simulacrum of thought or figment to relate…

Amid the lath and plaster and rubble-strewn
floors a mourning dove flutters, blessing the woeful
chambers with solemn song. And only now in this
lone vacuity is my skull cognizant of the lamp
of life and for one brief instant illumined...
Then to the celestial gyre my light passes beyond
all gravities, diffused in final prism to the stars...

Lamp of Life by Karl Ramberg

Melvin Litton's stories have appeared in *Chiron Review, Mobius, Foliate Oak, Floyd County Moonshine, Pif, First Intensity,* with poetry in *Broadkill Review, The Gasconade Review, The Literary Hatchet, Stray Branch,* and a chapbook *From the Bone* via Spartan Press. He has two published novels: *GEMINGA,* a man/raven fable concerning the Shining Path in Peru (III Publishing, 1993); and *I, JOAQUIN,* a fictional memoir of the Gold Rush bandit, Joaquin Murrieta, as told by his head encased in alcohol (Creative Arts Book Co., 2003) – both available in new editions from Crossroad Press. His third novel, *CASPION & The White Buffalo,* a saga of the American West, is forthcoming in 2018, again from Crossroad Press. He is a retired carpenter and lives in Lawrence, KS with his wife Debra and their black and tan shepherd Jack. He also writes and performs songs solo and with the Border Band: wwwborderband.com

www.ingramcontent.com/pod-product-compliance
Lightning Source LLC
Chambersburg PA
CBHW020127130526
44591CB00032B/555